MW00790346

AMERICAN CARDINAL READERS

For Catholic Parochial Schools

PRIMER

EDITOR OF LOWER GRADE READERS
EDITH M. McLAUGHLIN
Former Critic Teacher, Parker Practice School,
Normal School, Chicago, Ill.

EDITOR OF UPPER GRADE READERS
T. ADRIAN CURTIS, A.B., LL.B.
District Superintendent, formerly Principal, Alexander Hamilton
Junior High School, New York

ASSOCIATE EDITORS

SISTER MARY AMBROSE, O.S.D., A.M.
(Supervisor)
St. Joseph's College and Academy,
Adrian, Michigan

SISTER MARY GERTRUDE, A.M.
Former Supervisor of Parochial High Schools,
Sisters of Charity, Convent Station,
New Jersey

TAN Books
Gastonia, North Carolina

Nihil Obstat:

Arthur J. Scanlan, S.T.D.
Censor Librorum

Imprimatur:

✠ Patrick Cardinal Hayes
Archbishop of New York

New York, July 27, 1927

American Cardinal Readers were originally published in 1950 and reprinted in 2013 by Neumann Press, an imprint of TAN Books.

Typesetting and minor revisions and corrections in *American Cardinal Readers Primer* © 2021 TAN Books

ISBN: 978-0911845-52-5
Kindle ISBN: 978-1-5051-0521-6
ePUB ISBN: 978-1-5051-0808-8

Published in the United States by
TAN Books
PO Box 269
Gastonia, NC 28053
www.TANBooks.com

Printed in the United States of America

CONTENTS

GRANDMOTHER AND GRANDFATHER

This is Grandmother.
She is John's grandmother.
She is Jean's grandmother.
She is Baby's grandmother, too.

This is Grandfather.

He is John's grandfather.

He is Jean's grandfather.

He is Baby's grandfather, too.

This is a little farm.

It is Grandfather's farm.

Grandfather lives on this farm.

Grandmother lives on the farm, too.

GRANDMOTHER'S LETTER

One day Mother said,
"Here is a letter for you, John.
It is for you too, Jean.
The letter is from Grandmother."

"Please read it for us, Mother.
I can not read a letter," said John.

Mother said, "I will help you.
I will read the letter for you.

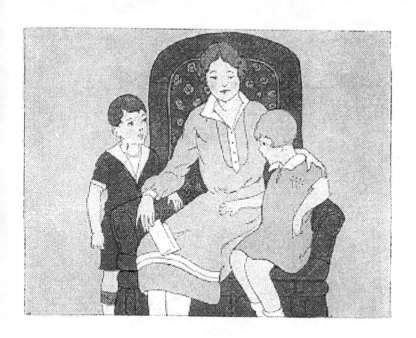

"'Dear John and Jean,
Grandfather wants to see you.
He wants to see Mother and Father.
He wants to see the baby.
I want to see you all, too.
Please come to the farm soon.
You can have a good time here.
                    Grandmother.'"

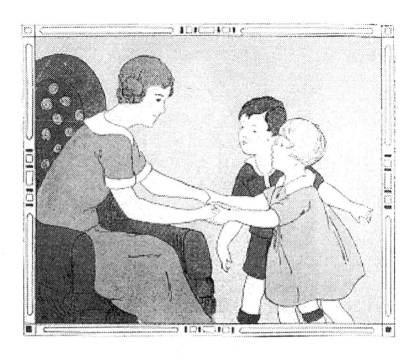

"May we go, Mother?" said Jean.
"I like to go to the farm."
John said, "I like the farm, too.
Please let us go, Mother.
We have a good time on the farm."
Mother said, "Let us ask Father.
He will come home soon."

Soon Father came home.

John said, "Here is a letter, Father.
It is from Grandmother.
She wants us to go to the farm.
Please may we go, Father?
Mother said to ask you."

Father said, "Let us all go.
Grandmother is good to ask us.
Tell Grandmother we will go, John."

John said to Father,
"I can not tell Grandmother that.
I can not write a letter."

Mother said, "Let me help you.
You can tell me what to write.
Then I will write it for you."

"I like to do that," said Jean.

John said, "I like to do that, too."

"Let us do it, then," said Mother.

Jean told Mother what to write.
John told Mother what to write.

This is what Jean and John said:

"Dear Grandmother,
We will go to the farm soon.
You are good to ask us to come.
We all want to see you.
We want to see Grandfather, too.
                    Jean and John."

WATCHING FOR FATHER

The next day Paul came to see John.

He came to see Jean, too.

John and Jean play with Paul.

Paul and John are good friends.

Jean and Paul are friends, too.

John said to Paul,
"We are going to the farm soon.
My grandmother lives on the farm.
My grandfather lives on the farm.
The train runs to the farm.
We are all going on the train."

Jean said to John and Paul,
"We are going on the train.
We are going on the train.
We are going to the farm
on the train."

Mother heard what John told Paul.
She heard what Jean told Paul.

Mother said to Jean and John,
"The train runs to the farm,
but we are not going that way."

Jean said, "What way are we going?
Please tell us, Mother, will you?"

Mother said, "Do not ask me to tell.
Father wants to tell you that.
He will come home soon."

Paul said,
"My father will come home soon, too.
It is time for me to go.
Good-by, Jean and John.
Good-by to you all."

Jean and John said, "Good-by, Paul.
Come and play with us soon."

Mother said, "Good-by, Paul.
You are a good boy.
You go home on time."

Then Paul ran home.

John ran out to watch for Father.
Jean ran out to watch, too.
She ran out with John.

John said, "You watch that way, Jean.
Father may come home that way.
I will watch this way.
He may come home this way."

John watched this way.
Jean watched that way.

Soon Jean saw a big car.

She saw Father in the big car.

"Here is Father! Here is Father!
He is in a big car," said Jean.

Jean ran to the big car.

Then John saw Father in the car.

He ran to the big car, too.

John said "I like this car. Father."

"I like the car, too," said Jean.

Father said, "I want you to like it. Can you tell why, Jean and John?"

"I can not tell why," said Jean.

"I can tell why! I can tell why! It is our car," said John.

"Yes, it is our car," said Father. "We are going to the farm in it."

Jean ran to Mother and said,
"The train runs to the farm,
but we are not going that way.
I can tell why! I can tell why!
We are going in our big car.
That is what Father told us."

Then Mother said to Jean,
"Yes, we are going in our car.
Father told me that, too."

WAKE UP!

One morning Jean did not wake up.

Mother said, "Wake up! Wake up, Jean!
Father and John are up.
The baby and I are up.
It is time for you to get up."

Jean did not wake up.

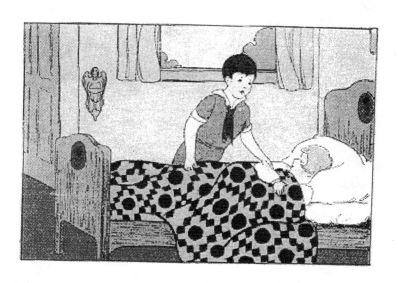

"Jean did not hear you, Mother.
She did not wake up," said John.

Mother said, "Please call her, John."

John called, "Wake up! Wake up!
Baby is up, but you are not.
You are a big girl, Jean.
It is time for you to get up.
Wake up! Wake up! Wake up!"

Jean did not wake up.

Father said, "Jean is not up.
She did not hear Mother call her.
She did not hear John call her.
I will call her this time.
I can wake her up."

Father called, "Wake up, Jean!
We are going to the farm.
We are going this morning.
We want you to go with us.
Wake up! Wake up, Jean!"

Then Jean did wake up.

JEAN'S MORNING PRAYER

Little Infant Jesus,
Bless my work and play.
All my love I give You;
Keep me good to-day.

BREAKFAST

Soon Jean ran to Mother and said,
"Good morning! Good morning!
I am glad to see you, Mother.
I am glad to see the baby, too."

Mother said, "Good morning, dear.
I am glad to see you, too."

Then Jean said to her mother,
"I want to help you this morning.
Please tell me what to do."

Mother said,
"Tell Father to come to breakfast.
Tell John to come to breakfast, too.
They are working this morning.
They are working on the car."

"I can tell why," said Jean.
"They want the car to go and go.
They want it to go to the farm."

"Yes, Jean, they do," said Mother.

Jean ran out to Father and John.

Father and John saw Jean.

"Good morning, Jean," said Father.

"Good morning, Jean," said John.

Jean said, "Good morning to you.
Will you please come to breakfast?"

"Here I come! Here I come!
I want my breakfast," said John.

"I do, too, Jean," said Father.

They all ran in to breakfast.

GRACE AT MEALS

We thank You, heavenly Father,
For all Your loving care;
And for the food You give us
Receive our grateful prayer.

A RIDE TO THE FARM

After breakfast Father said,
"It will soon be time to go.
Jean, you help Mother with her work.
You can help Mother too, John.
I will get the car.
Then it will be time to go."

Jean and John went to work.
Father went to get the car.

Soon Mother heard a horn.
Honk! Honk! Honk! it went.

Mother said, "I hear a horn.
It is the horn on our car.
Father wants us to come out.
It is time for us to go.
Are you ready, Jean and John?"

"I am ready, Mother," said Jean.

"I am ready too, Mother," said John.

John ran out to the car.

Jean ran out to the car.

She ran after John.

Then Mother came out with Baby.

Father helped Mother into the car.

He helped Jean into the car.

Then Father and John got in.

Father said, "Are you all ready?"

Mother said, "I am ready to go."

"I am ready too, Father," said Jean.

Then John said, "I am not ready.
I want Paul to go with us.
He is our good friend, Father.
Please may I ask him to go?"

Father said, "Yes, you may ask Paul.
I am glad you want him to go."

John ran to ask Paul.

Soon John ran back to the car.
Paul did not come back with him.

John said, "Paul is sick.
He can not go with us."

Mother said, "I am sorry he is sick."

"I am sorry for him, too," said Jean.

Father said, "I am sorry he is sick.
He may go with us the next time."

John got into the car.

Father said, "Are you all ready?
Are you ready to have the car go?"

"We are ready back here," said Mother.

"I am ready this time," said John.

"I am ready to go, too," said Father.

Then they all went to the farm.

A SURPRISE

The car was going on and on.
Jean was watching this way.
She was watching that way.
She was watching for the farm.

She said to her father,
"Father, is the farm far from here?"

"No, it is not far," said her father.
"It is the next one we come to."

Soon Father said, "We stop here.
This is Grandfather's farm."

Grandmother saw the car stop.
Grandfather saw it stop, too.

Grandmother said to Grandfather,
"Can you tell who is in that car?
They are calling to you and me."

Grandfather said,
"I can not tell who they are.
I can not see from here."

Grandmother said to Grandfather,
"Let us go out to the car.
I want to see who is in it."

Just then John got out of the car.
He ran up to the house.
Then Jean got out of the car.
She ran up to the house.
Father, Mother and Baby came next.
They walked up to the house.

34

Then Jean said to Grandmother,
"Did we surprise you, Grandmother?"

"Yes, you did, Jean," said Grandmother.
"I like you to surprise me this way."

Grandfather said,
"The car is a big surprise to me.
Please tell me all about it."

John told all about the car.
He told about the ride to the farm.

Grandmother said,
"You want a dinner after that ride.
It is time for dinner, too.
Come! You may all help me get it."

So they did.

ON THE FARM

After dinner Grandfather said,
"I am going out on the farm.
Do you want to go, children?"

"I want to go with you," said Jean.
"I want to see the farm animals."

John said, "I will go, Grandfather.
I want to see the animals, too."

The children went with Grandfather.

Jean said to Grandfather
"Please may we feed the animals?"

"I want to feed the animals, too.
I like to do that," said John.

Grandfather said, "Come with me.
I have good food for the animals.
The food is in the big barn.
Let us go to the barn for it."

They went to the barn for the food.

Then John said to Grandfather,
"Please tell us where to go first."

Grandfather said, "Jean is a girl.
Ask her to tell us where to go.
Girls come first, John."

Jean said, "Thank you, Grandfather.
I want to see the chickens first.
I like to feed the chickens.
They run to get what I have."

Jean went to feed the chickens.
Grandfather and John went with her.

"Come, chickens, come," said Jean.
"Here is good food for you.
This is corn I have for you.
Come and get this good corn."

The big chickens ran for the corn.
The little chickens ran, too.

Then Grandfather said to John,
"Where do you want to go, my boy?
What animals do you want to see?"
John said, "I like the cows.
The cows give us milk.
Milk is good for boys and girls."
"Let us go to see the cows then.
Come this way," said Grandfather.

John ran to the cows and said,
"I have good food to give you.
You give milk to us.
I want to give you this hay.
Jean wants to give you hay, too.
That is the way we thank you.
Come, cows! Come and get this hay."

The cows took the hay from John.
They took it from Jean, too.

Then Jean said to Grandfather,
"You took me to see the chickens.
You took John to see the cows.
We want to go with you this time."

Grandfather said,
"I have a surprise for you.
I have animals that give us wool.
Do you want to see them?"

Jean said, "I want to see them."

John said, "I want to see them, too.
I can tell they are sheep.
Sheep give us wool, Grandfather."

Grandfather said, "They are sheep.
Come with me to see them."

Jean ran to the sheep and said,
"Come, good sheep! Come to us!
You give wool to us all.
See what we have to give you!
Here are good big apples for you.
We want you to have them.
That is the way we thank you.
Come and get the big apples, sheep."

The sheep took the apples.

The children went to see Ned, then.
Ned is Grandfather's horse.

John ran up to Ned and said,
"Ned, you are a good horse.
You let Jean ride on your back.
You let me ride on your back.
We want you to have this apple.
That is the way we thank you."

Ned took the apple from John.

Grandfather said to the children,
"You saw all the animals we have.
You gave corn to the chickens.
You gave hay to the cows.
You gave apples to the sheep.
The horse got a good apple, too.
You gave all the animals good food.
That is one way to be kind to them.
Be kind to them in all ways.
Be kind to all animals.
God made them all."

BABY'S ANGEL

Grandfather went back to the house.
The children went back with him.

They went into the house.
Jean saw Grandmother there.
She saw her father and mother.
The baby was not there.

Jean said, "Where is the baby?
Did she go to sleep, Mother?"

Mother said to Jean,
"The baby is in Grandmother's bed.
She went to sleep after dinner.
It is time for her to wake.
She may be ready to get up.
Will you please go and see, Jean?"

"Yes, Mother, I will," said Jean.

Just then they all heard Baby cry.
Mother got up and ran to her baby.
Jean ran with her mother.
Grandmother walked after them.
On the way Mother called,
"Do not cry! Do not cry, Baby!
Here comes Mother to help you."

Mother and Jean ran into the room.
Jean saw a chair by the bed.
She saw the baby push the chair.

Jean said, "See Baby push the chair!
She wants to get out of this bed.
The chair is in her way, Mother.
See her push it from the bed!"

"I can see her push it," said Mother.
"Next time I will get a big chair."

49

Mother took Baby out of bed.

Grandmother came into the room.
She said, "What made the baby cry?
Did she fall out of my big bed?"

"No, she did not fall," said Jean.
"She wanted to get out of bed.
This chair was by the bed.
It was in Baby's way.
She pushed it and pushed it.
It did not go far from the bed.
So Baby did not fall."

Grandmother said to Jean,
"Baby's angel was watching her.
That is why she did not fall."

"That is so, Grandmother," said Jean.

PRAYER TO THE GUARDIAN ANGEL

Guardian Angel at my side,
Hear me when I pray;
Keep me free from every sin
All the night and day.

THE LITTLE ROUND HOUSE

John told Grandfather about Paul.
He told Grandmother about him, too.

John said, "My friend Paul is sick.
That is why he is not here.
May I take something home to him?
I want to surprise him."

Grandfather said to John,
"There is a house on this farm.
It is a house Paul will like.
You may take that to him."

John said to Grandfather,
"I can not take a house to him.
A house is too big to take."

Then Grandfather said,
"You can take this house, John.
Come! I will tell you about it.
Then you may go and find it."

John went out with Grandfather.

Grandfather said to John,
"The house is not far from here.
It is a little round house.
It is a house with no door.
It is a house with a star in it.
Go and look for it, my boy.
See if you can find this house."

John went to look for the house.

Just then Jean came out.
John called to her and said,
"Please come and help me, Jean.
I am looking for a house.
It is a little round house.
It is a house that has no door.
It is a house with a star in it.
I want to find this little house.
I want to take it to Paul."
Jean ran to help John.
They looked this way and that way.
They looked here and there.
They did not find the house.

Soon Father came out.

He saw Jean looking this way.

He saw John looking that way.

He called to them and said,

"What are you looking for, children?"

"We are looking for a house, Father.
Please help us find it," said John.
"It is a little round house.
It is a house that has no door.
It is a house with a star in it."

Father said, "Come with me, children.
I can help you find that house."

Father took the children to a tree.
"Look, children!   Look up!" he said.
"The round house is not far from you."

Jean looked up into the tree.
John looked up into the tree, too.
They saw good apples there.
"Father, is the apple the round house?
Is there a star in it?" said John.

"Ask Grandfather about that.
He will tell you," said Father.

Jean and John ran to Grandfather.

Jean said, "Look, Grandfather, look.
Father helped us find this apple.
Is it the little round house?"

John said, "The apple has no door.
Has it a star, Grandfather?"

"Let me help you," said Grandfather.

He took the apple and cut it.
There in the apple was a star.

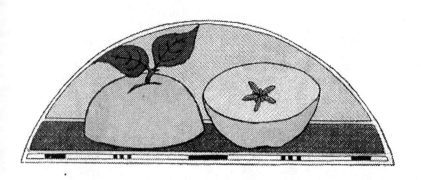

Jean and John saw the star.

John said to Grandfather,
"Now I can tell what the apple is.
It is the little round house.
It is the house that has no door.
It is the house with a star in it."

Grandfather said, "Yes, John, it is.
It is a house Paul will like, too.
Get one to take to him, John.
Jean, you get one for Paul, too."

So the children did.

GOING HOME

John found a big apple for Paul.
Jean found one for him, too.
Then Grandfather called to them,
"Come, children! Mother wants you."
Jean and John ran to Grandfather.
They went into the house with him.

"Here we are, Mother," said John.
"Grandfather told us you wanted us."
Mother said, "Yes, I do want you.
We must get ready to go home now."

"Please guess what I found, first.
It is something for Paul," said Jean.
"It is a round house with no door."

"I found a house like it," said John.
"You can guess what it is, Mother."

"I can not guess it," said Mother.
"You will have to tell me."

Jean was just going to tell Mother.
John looked at her and said,
"Do not tell, Jean! Do not tell!
You show Mother what you found.
I will show her what I found, too."

Then John showed Mother the apple.
"Look, Mother! Look at this!" he said.
"This is the little round house.
It is the house with the star."

Jean showed her apple to Mother.
"This is the house I found," she said.
"It is the house that has no door."

"What big red apples!" said Mother.
"Paul will be glad to get them.
Now, please get ready to go home."

Soon Jean and John were ready.
Mother and Father were ready, too.
Grandmother got the baby ready.
Grandfather took the baby in his arms.
Then they all went out to the car.

Father helped Mother into the car.
Grandfather gave the baby to her.
Jean and John got into the car.
Father got in and made the car go.
Then Grandfather called to them,
"Good-by! Good-by to you all."
"Come back soon," called Grandmother.
Then from the car they called,
"Thank you for the happy day.
Good-by! Good-by to you."

MOTHER'S STORY

The car was going on and on.
By and by John said to Mother,
"I like to go out to the farm.
I can have a good time there."

"I like to go there, too," said Jean.
"Then I can see my grandmother.
I can see my grandfather, too.
They are so good and kind to us."

"They love us all," said Mother,
"That is why they are so kind to us."

John looked at Mother and said,
"Grandmother loves Jean and me.
She loves our dear little baby.
Grandfather loves us all, too.
You and Father love us best."

"Father and I love you," said Mother.
"So do Grandmother and Grandfather.
There is One who loves us all.
His love is the best love.
He helps us to love one another."

"Mother, it is dear Jesus." said John.

"Yes, my boy, Jesus loves you best.
He loves little children," said Mother.
"I can tell you a story about that."

"Please tell us the story," said Jean.

So Mother did.

This is the story Mother told.

"God has a happy home for us all.

The happy home is called Heaven.

God sent Jesus to tell us about it.

He sent Him to help us get there.

God sent Jesus as a little Baby.

He sent Him to Mary and Joseph.

Baby Jesus grew and grew and grew.
He soon grew to be a big Boy.
He helped all children then.
He showed them how to please God.
He did what God wants them to do.
He loved His Mother and His Father.
He did just as He was told to do.
He did it in a happy way.
He loved His little friends, too.

Jesus grew to be a Man.
He went out to talk to the people.

He went from place to place.
He went to one place.
He talked to the people there.
Then He went to another place.
He talked to the people there.

Jesus told the people about Heaven.
He told them how to please God.

He said to the people,
'You must all love God.
You must love one another, too.
Then Heaven will be your home.'

One day Jesus was going to talk.
A good mother heard about it.
She said, 'How happy I am!
Jesus is going to talk to-day.
He will talk in a place near by.
He will pass this way to get there.
I will tell the mothers about it.
We must take the children to Him.
Dear Jesus will bless them.'

The mothers watched for dear Jesus.
The children watched for Him, too.

By and by one mother saw Him.
'Look! There is Jesus!' she said.
'He has some friends with Him.'

The mothers and children looked.
They saw Jesus and His friends.

Jesus walked as far as a big tree.
The mothers saw Him stop there.
They saw His friends stop, too.

'Jesus has to rest,' said a mother.
'He is going to rest by that tree.
Let us take the children to Him.
Jesus will be glad to see them.
He will bless them all.'

The big children ran to see Jesus.
The mothers took the little ones.
They were all so happy!

Soon they were near the big tree.
Jesus' friends saw them there.
They said, 'Go away! Go away!
Jesus can not talk to you now.
He must have this time to rest.'

All the children walked away.
The good mothers walked away.
They were not happy.

Jesus heard what His friends said.
He was not pleased with them.

Jesus saw the mothers going away.
He saw the children going away.
He looked at His friends and said,
'Let the little ones come to Me.
Do not tell them to go away.'

The mothers heard what Jesus said.
They took the children back to Him.

Dear Jesus loved the children
He called them all to Him.
He took one in His arms.

He told the children about Heaven.
He told them about God's love.
How happy they all were!

'We love You, Jesus,' said the children.
'I love you all,' said dear Jesus."

BACK HOME

Mother's story was over.

"I like that story," said Jean.

"Thank you for telling it, Mother."

"I like the story, too," said John.

Just then the car came to a stop.

"Why do we stop here?" asked John.

"Look at that house," said Father.

"Can you tell me who lives there?"

John looked and saw his home.

"Why, this is where we live," he said.

"Are you surprised?" asked Father.
"I am surprised, Father," said John.
"I did not know where we were.
I was watching Mother all the time.
I did not see where we were going.
So I did not know we were home."

John had a good laugh about it.
He made Jean and Baby laugh.
He made Mother and Father laugh.
They went into the house laughing.

PAUL'S SURPRISE

The next day John said to Mother, "May we go over to Paul's house? Jean and I want to surprise Paul. We want to give him the apples." "Yes, you may go," said Mother.

The children took the big apples. Then they ran over to Paul's house.

Paul's mother came to the door.

"Good morning, children," she said.

"Good morning," said Jean and John.

"Please may we see Paul?" asked John.

"Jean and I have a surprise for him.

It is something from the farm."

"Come in," said Paul's mother.

"Paul is not sick this morning.

He will be so glad to see you."

So the children went in.

Paul's mother called to him,
"Your little friends are here, Paul.
They have come to see you."

Paul ran to see Jean and John.

"Hello, John! Hello, Jean!" he said.
"Please tell me all about the farm.
Did you have a good time there?"

"Yes, we had a good time," said John
"We saw the animals on the farm.
Grandfather let us feed them.
Then we found something for you."

Then Jean said to Paul,
"Put out your hands,
    but do not look at them.
Put out your hands.
See what we put in them!"
Paul put out his hands.
The apples were put into them.
"Surprise! Surprise!" called John.
Paul looked and saw the apples.
"Thank you, Jean and John," he said.
"You gave me a good surprise."
Jean and John went home happy.

HELPING THE BIRDS

One day Mother called Jean to her.
"I want you to help me," she said.
"I want you to play with the baby."

"Will you put Baby near the window?
She likes to look out," said Jean.
"I like to look out the window, too."

"The window is a good place, Jean.
I will put Baby there," said Mother.
So she did.

Jean looked out and saw some birds.
She watched them fly here.
She watched them fly there.
Then she called to her Mother,
"There are some birds out here.
They are flying all over.
They must be looking for food."
Mother came to look at the birds.
"They are looking for food, Jean.
They can not find it," said Mother.
"Can we help them?" asked Jean.
"I will see, Jean," said Mother.
Then she went away.

Soon Mother came back.
Jean saw something in her hands.
"I found some good food for birds.
Here it is, Jean," said Mother.

Jean looked and saw bird seed.
There were some crumbs, too.

"That is good bird food," said Jean.
"Put some on the window sill.
Then we can see the birds find it."

Mother put seed on the window sill.
She put some crumbs there, too.

Mother, Jean and Baby watched.
One bird came to the window sill.
Then another and another came.
Soon all the birds were there.

"The birds are happy now," said Jean.
"They have found some good food."

Mother said to Jean,
"The days are getting cold now.
The birds can not find food.
We must put food out for them."

Jean put food out every day.

WHAT JEAN HEARD

One day John had been playing.
He had been playing with Paul.
Jean had been playing with them.

When playtime was over, Jean said,
"Our house is not far from here.
Come, John! Let us run to it.
Let us see who can get there first."

"Come over to this big tree, then.
Let us start from here," said John.

Jean went over to the tree.
She and John got ready to run.
"I am ready to go," said Jean.
"Tell me when to start, John."
"One, two, three! Go!" said John.

Away ran Jean and John.
They ran and ran and ran.
John got to the house first.

John and Jean ran into the house.
They heard some one talking.

"That is not Mother," said Jean.
"Let us go and see who it is."

"No, we must not do that," said John.
"Mother may not want us in there."

Mother heard Jean and John talking.
"You may come in, children," she said.
"Come and see who is here."

The children ran into the room.

Grandmother was in the room.
Grandfather was there, too.
They were glad to see the children.
The children were glad to see them.

Grandmother gave a book to Jean.
She said, "This is for John and you.
It is from Grandfather and me."

"Thank you! Thank you!" said Jean.
"You are so kind to us," said John.

John and Jean looked at the book.
Soon John said, "I know this story.
It is about the first Christmas.
I can read it for you, Grandmother."

"Let us all hear the story, John.
Please read it," said Grandmother.

So John did.

THE FIRST CHRISTMAS

There is a place called Bethlehem.
It is far away from here.

There are hills near Bethlehem.
Sheep go up and down the hills.
They find their food there.

At night they rest on the hills.
The shepherds watch them.

Long ago some shepherds watched.
They watched night after night.

One night they saw a light.
The light was in the sky.
What a bright light it was!
It made the night look like day.

The shepherds were afraid.

94

Soon an angel came.
The angel said to the shepherds,
"Do not be afraid.
I have come to tell you something.
You will be happy to hear it."

The shepherds were not afraid then.
They listened for the glad news.

The angel said to them,
"Jesus is born this night.
You will find Him in Bethlehem.
He is in a stable there.
He is with Mary, His Mother."

Many angels came in the sky then.
The shepherds heard them sing:
"Glory to God,
Glory to God."

Then the angels went away.
The light went from the sky.
The shepherds were alone.

Soon one of the shepherds said,
"Let us all go to Bethlehem.
Let us find dear little Jesus."

The shepherds went to Bethlehem.
They found dear Jesus in the stable.
He was with Mary, His Mother.
Saint Joseph was with them.

The shepherds were happy now.
They said, "God is good to us.
He has sent Jesus from Heaven.
He has sent Him to show us
the way there."

Then the shepherds thanked God.
They loved the Baby Jesus.
They went back to the hills happy.